Volume 2
Decodable
Reader

Mc
Graw
Hill
Education

Bothell, WA • Chicago, IL • Columbus, OH • New York, NY

Contents

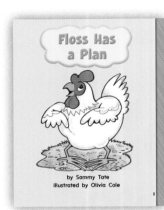

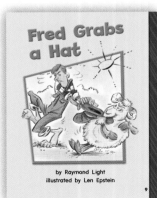

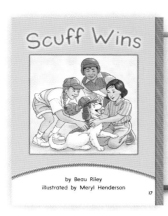

Floss Has a Plan

by Sammy Tate

illustrated by Olivia Cole

Floss sees a hut.
It is a mess.
But Floss likes it.
Can Floss fix it?

Floss has a plan.
Floss will ask Cliff.
"Can you fix this hut?" asks Floss.
Cliff will not fix it.

4

Floss is not glad.
Her plan is a flop!
Floss flaps and flaps.
But Cliff will not fix it.

Floss flaps and flaps.
She runs in the mud.
Floss is not glad!

Floss slips. Floss flops.
Floss flips over.
Floss is in the pail.
Floss can not get out!

Cliff runs to Floss.
Cliff will make a new hut.
Floss is glad.
This was her plan!

Fred Grabs a Hat

by Raymond Light
illustrated by Len Epstein

Brad is a trim man.
He is dressed in a trim hat.
He has a fat ram.
His fat ram is Fred.

Fred grabs Brad's hat.
Brad is mad.
"Drop this hat!" yells Brad.
Brad grabs his hat back.

Brad grips the brim.
Brad tugs and tugs.
Fred tugs and tugs, too.

Brad will not let Fred grab it.
But Fred will not budge.
Will Brad or Fred get the hat?

Brad slips!
Fred trips!
The hat flips!

Brad is a trim man.
Fred is a fat ram.
Now Fred has a fat hat!

Scuff Wins

by Beau Riley

illustrated by Meryl Henderson

Stef is up at bat.
"Hit it in!" yells Stan.
Will Stef hit the ball?

Stef hits it up, up, up!
Stan spins.
He is sticking his mitt up!
But he misses it.

Stan runs to get his ball.

He spots it.

It fell in!

Stan can not get it.

Stef tells Scuff to get the ball.
Scuff stops and looks up.
Will Scuff get it?

Scuff jumped in!
Scuff spots the ball.
He grabs it.
Scuff fixes it!

Scuff stops to drop the ball.
They pet Scuff.
"Scuff wins!" yells Stef.

Jen's Best Day

by Sally Ciardi

illustrated by Karen Tafoya

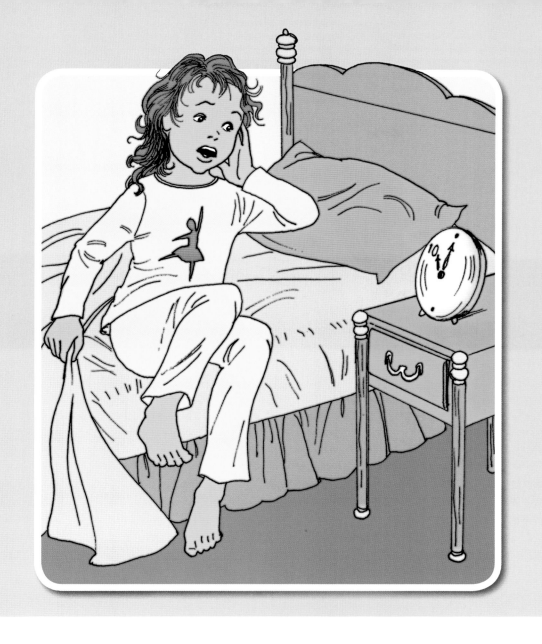

Jen jumps up.
"It is ten!" she yells.
"I must get to class!"

27

Jen's Mom says, "Stop!"
But Jen runs past.
"I must run!" says Jen.

"Will you stop and jump?"
asks Val.
"I must run!" gasps Jen.

Jen runs past the Yips.
"Have a drink," says Mr. Yip.
"I can not," yells Jen.
"I must run!"

"Can I help?" asks Mr. Buzz.
"It is past ten!" pants Jen.
"I just want to get in!"

"There is no class," he says.
"It is Saturday!"
"This is the best day," says Jen.
"I will run back and rest!"

Volume 2

Decodable Words

Target Phonics Elements: *l*-Blends

Cliff, flaps, flips, flop, flops, Floss, glad, plan, slips

High-Frequency Words

Review: *her, likes, make, new, sees, she, out, over, the, this, was, you*

Story Words

ask, pail

Decodable Words

Target Phonics Element: *r*-Blends

Brad, brim, dressed, drop, Fred, grab, grips, trim, trips

High-Frequency Words

Review: *and, he, now, or, this, the, too*

Story Words

budge

Decoding skills taught to date:
Phonics: Short *a*; Short *i*; Short *o*; Short *e*, Short *u*; *l*-Blends; *r*-Blends; *s*-Blends; End Blends

Structural Analysis: Plural Nouns -*s*; Inflectional Ending -*s*; Plural Nouns -*es*; Inflectional Ending -*es*; Closed Syllables; Inflectional Ending -*ed* (no spelling change); Inflectional Ending -*ing* (no spelling change); Possessives (singular)